Richard Walter Hart

SOAP MAKING
and
CANDLE MAKING
for Beginners

Step by Step Guide to Do-It-Yourself Soaps and Candles Recipes.

Table of Contents

Introduction

The book "Soap Making and Candle Making for beginners" is informative because it educates the reader on making soap and candles. It also teaches the reader how to use items found at home, saving money and time from buying new supplies. I would recommend reading this book for fun, not informational purposes.

The author wants to teach people how to make soap and candles. The author also wants to help people use items in their homes for soap and candle making, saving them money from purchasing new items from stores. They want the readers who read this book to have fun and learn about soap and candle-making at home.

The book "Soap Making and Candle Making" is excellent for anyone who wants to learn how to make soap and candles. Also, if you are interested in making your items rather than having to go out and purchase them, this book is for you. If you are a person who likes to spend time with family, try your hand at soap-making or candle-making with people using this book as a teaching tool.

This book has recipes for soap making and candle making. Try this today!

Chapter 1　Basics on Equipment and Safety in Organic Soap Making

The equipment you need in making your organic soap from scratch may just be lying around in your kitchen, so you may not need to head to specialty shops and start buying items from them. You can also search for soap-making equipment in thrift shops first before spending on additional items. You don't have to spend so much to produce quality organic soaps; just make sure you have all the basics. It would help if you also prioritized your safety. Your family's, as soap making, is essentially a chemical process that requires great care.

Utensils

You will need the following utensils in making your organic soaps:

- **Whisk (Stainless Steel)**. It is required when you blend your essential oils and other additives.

- **Spatula (Silicone)**. A silicone spatula will help you get as much soap as possible from your mixing container.

- **Spoon (Stainless Steel)**. A stainless-steel spoon is suitable for mixing oils by way of stirring them.

- **Large Spoon (Stainless Steel)**. You will need a large spoon for efficiently and safely stirring lye and water together.

- **Strainer (Stainless Steel)**. Use a stainless-steel strainer to dispense lye water into the oils, and ensure that no lye lumps can mix into the soap blend.

Containers

Having plenty of containers is essential in soap making. Make sure you choose those made of heat-proof Ingredients (stainless steel is preferred, as it does not react chemically with soap or lye). You should also ensure that your soap-making containers are not used for any other purpose.

- **Water Container (Polypropylene, Glass, or Pyrex).** You will need a heat-resistant container for holding your water as well as measuring it. Use it to mix your lye solution as well.

- **Lye Granules Container (Polypropylene, Glass, or Pyrex).** You will this type of container to measure your lye granules.

- **Liquid Oils Container (Polypropylene).** A separate container is needed to measure your oils.

- **Container for Additional Ingredients (Polypropylene).** You will also need several small containers to measure tiny amounts of oils required for superfatting your soaps. These containers will also serve as helpful for measuring other ingredients such as your powders, essential oils, botanicals, and other additives.

- **Oil-Heating Container (Stainless Steel).** You need to have a deep pan made of stainless steel to heat your oils.

Molds

You may choose from a variety of molds that are available in different sizes and shapes.

- **Wooden Box**. Line a wooden box with wax paper, and you will instantly have a traditional soap mold. This type of mold may work best for a beginner in soap making like you. Using the wooden box as your soap mold will give you soap loaves that will later be cut up to yield individual bars of soap. Using the wooden box also gives you soaps that are insulated well enough to provide them with a uniform color.

- **Plastic Storage Bins**. Simple plastic storage bins can be used to mold your organic soaps.

- **Food Containers**. Use heat-resistant food containers as soap molds to help you save money.

- **Cardboard Box**. You may also line a cardboard box with freezer or wax paper taped to its inside surfaces to create a quick soap mold.

Immersion Blender

You will need this kitchen aid to induce your lye-water and oil to react with one another quickly. It helps to choose one with holes in its head to ensure that only a tiny amount of air is mixed into your soap blend, which helps prevent your soaps from having plenty of air bubbles in them.

Digital Thermometer

An essential part of soap making is the accurate measurement of the temperature of the lye water and oils. You may opt for a glass thermometer, although they tend to break easily. A digital thermometer is not only inexpensive, but it also cleans easily. It can be dipped into both your lye water and oils.

Digital Kitchen Scales

Digital kitchen scales are a must in making your organic soaps. They allow you to accurately measure weight, which is a more precise measuring volume than measuring in volume. Use kitchen scales to get consistent measurements each time.

Gloves, Goggles, and Other Protective Gear

Although making your organic soaps is an enjoyable activity, it requires you to handle lye, which is dangerous when not handled properly. Make sure to wear gloves and safety goggles when mixing lye, and do not remove them until after you are done with making your soaps. It is vital to keep them on, along with your long-sleeved shirt, close-toed footwear, long pants, and apron, even while cleaning up.

Chapter 2   The Basic Techniques and Ingredients

Classic Soap-making Techniques

Cold process soap-making is what most people think of when they hear the term soap-making, but other techniques are great fun and yield a wide variety of soaps.

Cold-Process Soap

Cold-process soap is the most common soap-making or soaping technique. Here you combine a sodium hydroxide solution (lye) with fatty acids (oils, butter, or fats), emulsify them together, and pour them into a mold. You can add scents, colors, and additives during this process. It can also be swirled, layered, stamped, and piped. The soap is then left to work its magic through the saponification process. During this time, cold-process soap goes through an exothermic reaction, which generates its heat. It is called cold-process soap because the soap maker adds no warmth. The chemical reaction of saponification usually occurs within 24 hours, and you are left with soap. Cold-process soap needs to cure for four to six weeks. This will ensure that most of the water has fully evaporated so the soap won't dissolve quickly.

Hot-Process Soap

Hot-process soap is like cold-process soap, except you heat the soap to force it through the saponification process. You can cook the soap in a slow cooker, double boiler, or oven.

Once the soap is cooked, you add essential oils, colorants, and additives. The soap is then spooned into a mold and left to harden. Once hard, your soap can be unmolded and cut. It is technically ready to use right away. However, hot-process soap still needs at least a two-week cure to allow some water to evaporate. One benefit to making hot-process soap is that the lye is no longer active when you add your essential oils. This means that you can usually use less essential oil than you would in cold-process soap, and the scents tend to come through more potent and more stable.

Liquid Soap

Liquid soap is made a lot like hot-process soap, except potassium hydroxide is used to saponify the oils. You bring your base oils and lye solution to "trace" (see **Recognizing Trace**) and then cook the mixture until it is neutral. The cloudy mixture turns translucent with an amber color, resulting in a liquid soap paste. You then dilute the paste and add essential oils for scent. Liquid soap is excellent for guest bathrooms and can be dispensed in a pump.

Melt-And-Pour Soap

Melt-and-pour is the best option for those who don't want to use lye. The soap base is made with lye, but it contains no active lye that you would have to handle. To make melt-and-pour soap, you purchase a melt-and-pour base, chop it up, gently melt it, and then add color, scent, and additives. You pour it into a mold, and as soon as it hardens, you can unmold it. Melt-and-pour soap is ready to use right away; no cure time is needed. It's a fun activity to do with children.

Hand-Milling Soap

Hand-milling is another excellent process for those who don't want to use lye. To make hand-milled soap, you either purchase or make an unscented cold-process or hot-process soap. Then you shred it and heat it to soften. Once it turns into a soap gel, you can add scent, additives, and color and then scoop it into a mold. Once it hardens, it can be unmolded and cut. Like hot-process soap, it is safe to use right away, but it benefits from a bit of a cure to allow the water to evaporate. Hand-milled soap isn't as smooth-looking as cold-process soap—it has a rustic look. Because the soap is so thick, it can be harder to create a design, but it can be layered and swirled to add interest. Hand-milling is also a great technique to re-batch (make again) a soap that didn't come out quite right.

Making natural soap at home is nothing short of a beautiful and creative adventure! But before you start gathering your ingredients, you need a solid foundation. Here you'll learn all about oils, butter, and measurements to start making your natural homemade soap. I'll also tell you about the essential oils you can use to make fragrance-filled soaps. But before we build that strong foundation, let's look at how soap is made.

When the oil used turns into salt due to the chemical reaction of lye and water, soap is made. This process is known as saponification. For cold process soaps to become saponified, it can take anywhere between 24 to 48 hours. Bar soaps cannot be made without alkalis, while liquid soaps cannot be made without potassium hydroxide. Alkalis and potassium hydroxide can be extremely dangerous if not used properly. To avoid any chemical reaction, you are advised to utilize all safety equipment and procedures throughout the entire process, as failure to do so can cause injuries. Wait until your kids are at school, your spouse at work, and your pets out of reach before you start making your natural homemade soap!

Basic Soap Ingredients

If you look at the packaging of a chemically made soap, you'll notice a scary list of ingredients. The beauty of homemade soap is that a simple bar requires very few. Of course, the optional components like fragrance, color, and embedded fruit pieces are nice to have; but here's what you need to make your first homemade bar of soap:

Lye

You already know that soap cannot be made without sodium hydroxide for bars and potassium hydroxide for liquid soaps. Lye will provide these ingredients. When you add lye to the water and dissolve it, there will be vapor. Don't inhale it.

Distilled Water

You shouldn't use regular water from the tap. Use distilled water as it helps to eliminate any contaminants along with high amounts of minerals that water might contain.

Borax

You know the dangers of high and low pH, and that's why you need borax. It helps to neutralize any leftover lye in liquid soaps, boosting its cleaning capacity. Borax is a natural ingredient mined from the earth. It is an excellent disinfectant and deodorizer.

Soap Colorants

The classification of colorants is based on their origin.

Natural Soap Colorants

Natural colorants are all completely natural products that can color soap, such as coffee, spices, decoctions, oils, and many others. In addition to giving color, they affect the skin positively by nourishing and cleansing it. Some of these colorants even have scrubbing properties

However, natural colorants have some disadvantages:

- The first major disadvantage is that such dye can migrate in soap, which causes one color to migrate into other layers of the soap. Migration is relevant for soaps of two or more colors. Over time, the color will simply change or become pale.

- Natural colorants also reduce the transparency of the soap base and make it slightly opaque.

- The shelf life of soaps with natural colorants is significantly shorter than any other type of soap. If you use juices or vegetables/fruits to create such soap, it may become moldy after a short time. If you add decoctions and dry herbs, store the soap in the refrigerator for no longer than 2–3 weeks.

However, the great advantage of colorants of natural origin is that you can make them from products you have at home. Now let's see what product exactly can give your soap the desired color.

<table>
<tr><th colspan="2" align="center">SOAP COLORS PRODUCTS</th></tr>
<tr><td>RED</td><td>Madder root, red clay, paprika, Brazilian clay, alkanet tinctoria, red sandalwood powder</td></tr>
<tr><td>ORANGE</td><td>Tomato paste, buriti oil, carrot juice, rosehip oil, annatto seeds</td></tr>
<tr><td>YELLOW</td><td>Sea buckthorn oil, turmeric, mustard oil, saffron, calendula or daisy flowers, daffodil flowers, goldenrod, lemon zest</td></tr>
<tr><td>GREEN</td><td>Spirulina, spinach, rosemary, parsley juice or barley extract, unrefined bay oil, chlorophyll, sage, henna powder</td></tr>
<tr><td>BLUE</td><td>Indigo, chamomile essential oil, blue clay, tinctorial wood</td></tr>
<tr><td>BLACK AND GREY</td><td>Charcoal, blue clay</td></tr>
<tr><td>BROWN</td><td>Chocolate, cocoa, crushed cloves</td></tr>
<tr><td>IVORY</td><td>Milk</td></tr>
<tr><td>PURPLE</td><td>Alkanna tinctoria, Gromwell Lithospermum erythrorhizon root</td></tr>
<tr><td>PINK</td><td>Madder root powder, hibiscus,</td></tr>
</table>

	lady's bedstraw, gallium verum, mahogany oil, sorrel rumex acetosa

Caution: If you add spices to the soap, be very careful, as they can cause allergies and a burning sensation.

The best way to give soap the color that you want is to use dry extracts. But they can only be used with the hot process. If you add them during the cold process of soap creation, the lye solution will destroy the color and nutrients.

Base Oils and Other Oil Types

Oils and Butters

These are essential ingredients required to make homemade soap. You probably know that each oil and butter have other properties, and each has different uses. For instance, lavender oil is for peace, whereas eucalyptus is for massaging joints. The base oils are lard, tallow, and palm oil. Cleansing oils are coconut, babassu, and palm kernel oil.

You can use castor oil for added lather and moisture. Apart from these oils, you can use many others to add conditioning ability to your soap.

Fragrances

What if I told you that you could easily make your scented soap? To do this, you need to know only a few standard rules for making such soap and when to add scents so that they remain longer in the finished product.

Fragrances can be divided into three main groups:

- Cosmetic fragrances
- Fragrance compositions
- Essential oils

The most natural is essential oils, which will give your soap a pleasant scent and valuable qualities. The total amount of essential oils in ounces/grams should not be more than 3% of the total mass of the soap. Also, note that some essential oils should not be more than 1%- 2% of the soap. Take caution.

Essential oils have significant advantages:

- They are natural.
- They do not thicken the soapy mass.
- They do not react with lye.

But they are fragile. This means that after a couple of months, your soap will be completely odorless.

Tip: In the box where the soap is stored, put a piece of cotton wool soaked in essential oil, and over time, the soap will absorb the smell (the p*art* of the cotton wool can be periodically re-soaked).

Other Additives

Soap additives are not only vegetables and essential oils but also various fillers. To make your soap look even more natural, use dried flowers, herbs, spices, clay, and honey.

They will make your soap not only helpful but also beautiful and fragrant.

To add various flowers and herbs to the soap, they must first be dried and ground up.

Marigold petals should be pre-crushed. If they are added to the soap, they will acquire a golden orange color. And the beneficial properties of calendula will improve skin color and condition. Calendula has anti-inflammatory, wound-healing, and tonic effects.

Chamomile flowers give the soap a strong aroma. They must first be crushed, or you can make an infusion and add one tablespoon to the soap. Chamomile has anti-inflammatory, hemostatic, and antiseptic effects.

Scrub Additives. To give the soap the properties of exfoliation, you can add to it various natural components.

Chapter 3   Candle Making Fundamentals

The Techniques of Candle-Making

The process of making candles is relatively simple. As long as you have the right ingredients, it should be straightforward for you to do some molding. However, depending on the candle that you are planning to make, you might want to use one of the two processes:

The Art of Candle Dipping

Candle dipping has probably been one of the first techniques used to make candles, which remained throughout the centuries. You don't even need a mold with this technique – you need a wick and the melted wax. It is generally the technique used to make taper candles, but it may be used for other candle types.

This method means that you will continuously dip the wick into the melted wax, pulling it up, letting it dry for a few seconds, falling it in again. You repeat the process until you get the right thickness of your candle. The method may be frightening – and time-consuming – but this might provide better and more creative designs in some cases.

For instance, you may start with a white or ivory base – after which you add two three layers of red, two three layers of yellow, and so on. Once all the layers have been set, you can begin carving the candle – and the result will be a colorful masterpiece.

Bear in mind that you might want to go for softer wax if you wish to cut a candle. This way, it will not begin to crumble once you dig the knife in – and you'll be able to sculpt your candle in any way you want it.

The Simplicity of Mold Pouring

Pouring into the mold is likely one of the most popular ways to make candles, mainly because it's quick and stress-free. With the first method, you have to spend a lot of time dipping, dipping – and then dipping again. The process is not that quick, which is why we can see the appeal of just pouring some wax into a mold.

Once the wax has melted, you remove the candle from the mold – and it will be able to stand freely on its own. Plus, if you choose a soft wax, you will still be able to carve the candle into the shape you want.

The beauty of molds is that you can find them in various shapes and sizes – so, if you want a Darth Vader, there is a high chance that you might be able to come across such a candle mold.

Bear in mind that the candles made in the mold will require you to place them on a plate or candle support. They can also be introduced in the lantern – but remember that you will also need something to collect any stray wax.

Pouring into Containers

Suppose you want candle-making to be even more simplistic. In that case, you may adopt the technique of pouring the wax into containers. They can be glass cups, glass jars, or other containers that you may believe in fitting a candle.

The advantage of containers is that you will no longer have to bother pulling the candle out once it has hardened. You can leave them there and light them whenever you need them. You won't even need a plate or candle support, mainly because the melted wax will remain in the jar.

Make sure that the container you purchase is resistant to high temperatures – particularly around 140 degrees Fahrenheit. Some glass recipients will crack under this temperature – which is why you have to ensure that they will resist. Moreover, you must ensure that the interior margins of the jar are smooth. If not, you risk the wax contracting and hardening improperly – causing the surface to be rather unsightly.

Pouring into containers takes the least time – mainly because all you have to do is melt the wax, add the wick in the container, and pour the wax. Once everything is over and done with, you may light the candle and proceed to set the mood.

The Steps to Creating Your Candles

Candles represent one of the best ways to bring some fragrance and light into a room. At the same time, they can become an enjoyable DIY project. Once you have gathered all of the ingredients and have crafted an idea in your head, it is time you start your candle-making process.

This example will be for a standard candle-in-a-jar. However, you may replace the jar with a mold if you have some other unique ideas in mind. From the beginning to the end, here is how you make a candle.

Step 1: Decide on the Wax

At this point, you should decide what type of wax you want to use for your candles. As you have seen, there are several types that you can choose from – from paraffin to beeswax and soy. Paraffin is generally the most popular, mainly because it's cheap – buy soy and beeswax are the better choices if you want more malleability. The latter options are also renewable, which means you won't have to buy the entire amount of wax on and on.

Step 2: Prepare the Area

Unless you don't care whether wax gets on the surface of your workspace or not, you should protect it with a newspaper or something similar. If you are working on tile or granite, it should not necessarily be a problem. However, if the area gets easily stained, you must protect it.

Plus, you need to consider the cleaning aspect. Indeed, the wax will not stain tile or granite, and you can clean it – but once the wax hardens, you will wish that you went through the trouble of protecting your workspace. Once you have to start scrubbing the area – and realize that the wax won't go away quickly – you'll understand why a simple piece of the newspaper goes a long way. When you are done, you toss the paper into a trash can, and you are done with everything.

Step 3: Cut the Wax into Chunks

When you are buying wax, you'll likely be getting it in a more significant block. While it may seem tempting to save yourself the bother and drop the entire block into the double boiler, you might want to take the time and cut it into shavings or chunks. This way, you will make sure that the wax will melt at a nice and even rate.

Step 4: Use the Double Boiler

You can go two ways around this: one, you can buy a double boiler that is specifically designed for melting wax – or you can make your double boiler at home.

For the sake of looking after our budget, let's say that you decided on a DIY double boiler. In this case, you will want to take a large pot – and then fill it with water halfway.

You will have to place a smaller container in that large container filled with water – a heat-resistant one. Once the water inside the main container starts boiling, it will heat the contents of the minor recipient – and then the wax will boil.

Bear in mind that wax may be rather tricky to clean – which is why you have to pick a small container that you will use exclusively for candle making. Do not boil directly over the fire – otherwise, the wax might evaporate or catch fire.

Step 5: Keep an Eye on the Thermometer

Depending on the wax you are using, you should keep an eye on the temperature of the resin. Each different type of wax will reach its melting point at different temperatures. Here are the temperatures at which the waxes should be fully melted:

- **Paraffin Wax:** 122-140 degrees Fahrenheit
- **Soy Wax:** 170-180 degrees Fahrenheit
- **Beeswax:** 145-170 degrees Fahrenheit
- **Recycled Wax:** 185 degrees Fahrenheit

Once the temperature has been reached, you may move onto the next step.

Step 6: Add Scents

Once the wax has melted, it is time for you to add the scents. You may find scents in various places – and the choice should be up to your preferences. You may go for a scent you particularly like, or you may choose it based on the effects of aromatherapy. Lavender, for instance, is an excellent option if you are feeling stressed out or dealing with anxiety.

Bear in mind that every fragrance bottle will come with instructions regarding its concentration. Ideally, you might want to read the label first – and not just "wing it" by adding it directly into the wax. Remember that you also have to stir well so that the fragrance can mix into the wax.

Step 7: Add the Coloring

The regular food coloring will not work when it comes to candles, mainly because it is water-based. However, you can hit the craft store and find some oil-based dye. You may even find candle dye specifically for your type of wax. All you have to do is add a few drops of color – and stir until everything evens up. Add until you reach the color that you want.

Step 8: Add the Wick into the Container

Take a bamboo stick or a pencil and attach the top of the wick to it. Place the stick over the container, and let the wick drop down to the bottom. Make sure that the wick is placed straight into the center of the mold or container.

At this point, you may use any kind of container: a jar, an old teacup, a metal tin – practically anything that you know for sure can withstand the heat. As long as it won't break down under high temperatures, it will be good to go.

Step 8: Pour the Melted Wax

Once everything has been set, you may pour the melted wax into the container or the mold. In this case, you will be the judge of how much wax will go into the mold. If you are using beeswax, bear in mind that it will shrink.

Step 9: Allow the Wax to Cool

This will once more depend on the type of wax that you are planning to use. For example, soy wax and beeswax can take 4-6 hours to cool down, whereas paraffin will take around 24 hours. As a rule of thumb, the longer you allow it to cool, the better.

Once it has been cooled down, cut off the excess wick. If you used a mold, remove it. If you placed it in a jar or container, then leave it that way.

Step 10: Light It Up

Now that your masterpiece is done, all you have to do is light the wick and enjoy. Depending on the wax type and quantity you have used, you should last for a couple of hours.

While this is generally the standard way of making a candle, remember that the process is up for customization. Let's take the dyeing process as an example: you may swirl just a few colors in the mix and only stir slightly to get a few traces. This way, you will get a multicolor candle that will be very interesting to look at. Candle making is an art – and every artist should have the freedom of creating his models.

Chapter 4   Different types of candle wax

You know how candles were made back in the day and what you need to make candles? Let's start candle-making. The first step in creating a candle is to understand the candle wax.

Wax and wicks are two primary ingredients for a candle. The rest of the things are just additives to make specialized candles. There are different kinds of candle wax. The type of wax you choose depends on the type of candle you want to make. The candle wax determines various melting points and reactions to the additives like fragrance and color.

Different types of wax have other melting points. Generally speaking, soft wax has a low melting point, and hard wax has a high melting point. While buying candle wax, you should always check the type of wax, the melting point, and the reaction to the additives (if any).

Here are some common waxes used for candle making.

Paraffin

Paraffin is the most common candle wax. It is also the cheapest wax available on the market. Paraffin is derived during the refining of petroleum. If you are just beginning to make candles, you should work with paraffin. Making candles from paraffin will teach you a lot about how to make candles.

The melting point for paraffin wax has a wide variation. Paraffin has low, moderate as well as high melting points. Because of this variation, you can make various types of candles from paraffin.

You can also use paraffin wax to make candles with snowflakes effects and crystal patterns. Paraffin gives you a kind of flexibility that no other wax will provide you with.

Pros:

- Paraffin is the cheapest candle wax. Therefore, you can make many candles on a small budget.
- Paraffin is the best candle wax for beginners.
- You can make decorative candles from paraffin.
- You can use any type of candle dye.
- You can use any kind of candle fragrance.
- You can use any kind of additives.

Cons:

- Paraffin is not environmentally friendly as it is derived from oil mining.
- Paraffin is non-biodegrade.

Cream Wax

Paraffin does not contain natural oils. However, when paraffin is mixed with natural oils, the wax we get is cream wax. Cream wax contains mineral oil and resin compounds. Cream wax is clean. It burns consistently, without any interruptions, such as bubbles. It has a high melting point. Therefore, there will be no soot left (black ash against the glass jar).

Cream wax is solid yet soft. If you want to make scented candles, cream wax is better than paraffin wax. Cream wax makes the best container candles. Sadly, you cannot make a tapered candle with cream wax.

Pros:

- Cream wax is the best option for a container candle.
- Cream wax is suitable for beginners.

Cons:

- It can be used only for container-based candles.

Gel Wax

Gel wax is derived from mineral oils. Typically, gel wax is used for themed candles. It is clear, and even if you use dyes, it remains see-through. Gel wax is also odorless.

You can embed various decorative objects – for instance, a glass fish or glitters – in a gel candle. Gel wax has an opaque appearance and does not easily mix with additives. Gel wax has a high melting point.

Gel wax is different from paraffin wax or vegetable wax. Interestingly, you cannot make tapered candles with gel wax; you have to pour the gel wax into a container to make candles. If you want to use scents, you have to choose fragrance wisely because gel wax does not support all kinds of fragrance oils.

Since gel wax has a high melting point, it generates high temperatures. If you are using a thin glass container for gel wax, your container might crack.

Pros:

- Gel wax is the ideal choice for decorative candles.
- You can use gel wax to make candles with various designs like glitters, floating beads, underwater scenes, etc.
- You can make a collectible candle from gel wax.
- Gel candles burn slowly, making your candle last longer.
- Gel wax candles are easier to handle.

Cons:

- You cannot use cotton wicks because cotton does not burn well in gel candles.
- You need to choose the container for the gel candle wisely as it might crack.
- Gel wax candles create bubbles while burning.

Soy Wax

Soy is a beneficial plant. It is the ultimate source of protein for vegetarians and vegans. Soy can be used in many ways. You can use soybeans as food and also make milk, tofu, oil, and wax.

Using soy for a candle is quite a recent discovery. When soybean oil is hydrogenated, we get soy wax. Since soy wax comes from soybean oil, it has natural oils. Thus it blends very well with natural additives and natural fragrance oils. Soy wax has different melting points, which differ according to the additives used. You can use soy wax to make a variety of candles.

Pros:

- It is comparatively inexpensive.
- The wax burns clearly.
- Since soy is plant-based wax, unlike paraffin, soy wax is a sustainable resource.
- Good for the environment because, unlike paraffin, it does not do any environmental damages.
- Soy wax is biodegradable.
- It is easy to clean soy wax when it spills on something. No carcinogenic chemical is required.
- The best wax to make large candles.

Cons:

- It is hard to mix some chemical fragrance oils with soy wax because soybean oil does not hold all types of fat.
- Soy wax does not easily hold dyes. Therefore, you need to find shades especially made for soy wax.
- Making candles from soy wax is not for beginners.
- Soy wax burns faster.

Palm Wax

Palm wax is a plant-based wax; it is derived from palm trees. Palm wax has a long burning time, the longest all of the plant-based wax. Palm wax produces a bright flame, much more colorful than most of the other waxes. Palm wax candles do not produce smoke. It has a high melting point. Therefore, it is best used in hot climates.

Pros:

- Since palm wax is plant-based wax, it does not harm the environment.
- It is biodegradable. Thus, it is environment-friendly.
- Best candle wax for long-lasting candles.

Cons:

- Very expensive.
- It can be very challenging to work with.

Bayberry Wax

The fruits of the bayberry plant are naturally coated with wax. Also called candleberry, the bayberry wax is derived by boiling the berries from this plant. When bayberries are boiled, wax collects on the top, and it is then scraped and collected. The bayberry wax has green pigmentation; therefore, you do not have to use green dyes to make green candles. The wax has a sweet, floral smell. Thus, it is ideal for making scented candles.

Comparatively, bayberry wax is expensive. One of the reasons why the bayberry wax is costly is because it takes a lot of time to make wax from bayberries. They are generally used during special occasions like Christmas and New Year.

Pros:

- Traditionally, bayberry candles are thought to bring fortune and prosperity.
- It has a natural aroma.
- Environmentally friendly, as it comes from natural sources.

Cons:

- The bayberry wax must be mixed with other plant-based wax to make strong bayberry candles, usually beeswax.
- This is an expensive option for candle wax.

Beeswax

As the name suggests, beeswax is made by honeybees. It is found in honeycombs. Beeswax is yellow or brown and has a sweet smell. The wax burns slower and releases aroma as it burns. Beeswax has a high melting point.

Pros:

- It has a natural aroma
- Burns slow
- Gives white light instead of yellow flame.
- Environment-friendly.
- Ideal candle wax for making hand-sculpted candles.

Cons:

- Due to the presence of honey, scent, and fragrance, oils do not readily mix with beeswax.
- More on the expensive side
- Due to its sticky nature, cleaning can be difficult if it spills on the carpet or clothes.

Tallow Wax

The first proper candles, the candles made from wax and wick, were made from tallow wax. Tallow is the wax derived from animal fat. Fat from domestic animals such as sheep, pigs, and cattle was used as candle wax for a long time until spermaceti was discovered in the 18th century and paraffin in the 19th century. Spermaceti is also animal-based fat. However, unlike fat, spermaceti does not smoke or odor while burning.

Tallow wax does not have color and has a low melting point

Pros:

- People made candles from tallow for hundreds of years.

Cons:

- Emits smoke while burning
- It gives a foul odor when burned.

Chapter 5   Soap Making Recipes

Jade Swirl

Ingredients:

- Loaf Mold
- Hanger Swirl Tool
- 3.2 ounces Borage Oil
- 1.2 ounces Castor Oil
- 10 ounces Coconut Oil
- 17.6 ounces Olive Oil
- 8 ounces Palm Oil
- 5.6 ounces Sodium Hydroxide Lye
- 11.9 ounces Distilled Water
- 2 ounces Jade Fragrance Oil
- 1.5 teaspoons Titanium Dioxide
- One teaspoon Aqua Pearl Mica
- ½ teaspoon Kelly Green Mica

Directions:

1. Make your first colors ready. In a liquid oil, place one teaspoon Aqua Pearl Mica. Add a lightweight liquid oil of your choice to the Kelly Green Mica and a half tablespoon.
2. Add lye to the water and mix until transparent and the lye is dissolved.
3. Cast the oils and mix. To support the bumps, use the stick mix.
4. Cool lye and oils to 130°F and then combine and stick to obtain a thin trace.
5. Whisk to the whole combination.
6. Put approximately 500 ml in a smaller container.
7. The bottle of soap is slightly darkened. Whisk and mix well.
8. Into the mold, pour the green soap. Then, pour a few of the white soap into the top mold, which will help it penetrate the green soap.
9. To saturate the mold, use alternative soaps. In a new batch, tap the mold to release the air bubbles. Sprinkle the soap briskly to maintain it.
10. Allow the soap to be made up of green and white swirls.
11. Tap forcefully to remove bubbles of air.
12. Insert the Swirl Tool and construct loops in the middle of the mold. In the mold, the height continues to increase. More incredible loops mean more turbulences. You have to do what you do. Sweat pulls and rolls along the mold's side.
13. Spread in a straight line the white and green soap along the top.
14. To prevent soda ash, ventilate the top.
15. Keep the mold-covered and insulated. Every 30 minutes, check your soap to make sure that it isn't too hot and cracking.
16. Mold the soap off for two to three days. Continue.
17. For four to six weeks, heal the soap bars.

Simple Black Tea

Ingredients:

- Mold with a sliding bottom
- Silicone Liner
- 2.7 ounces Cocoa Butter
- 13.5 ounces Coconut Oil
- 2.7 ounces Matcha Green Tea Butter
- 16.2 ounces Olive Oil
- 13.5 ounces Palm Oil
- 5.4 ounces Sweet Almond Oil
- 14.3 ounces Brewed Black Tea
- 7.6ounces Sodium Hydroxide Lye
- 2 ounces Bergamot Black Tea Fragrance Oil
- Three teaspoons Titanium Dioxide
- One teaspoon Activated Charcoal
- Three teaspoons Purple Brazilian Clay
- Black Tea Leaves

Directions:

1. Begin with color preparation into the liquid oil you want three cubic tabs of titanium dioxide. Mix the charcoal with one tablespoon of liquid oil in a separate container. Finally, combine three tabletops of distilled water in a third container with the purple Brazil clay.
2. Boil your brewed black tea with 16 ounces of distilled water. Let the tea be cold and steep for around an hour. Wait for a fantastic tea to about 70 degrees — the harder the tea, the clearer the lye blend. The tea can also be frozen and prepared as you would the method for milk soap.
3. Slowly and be careful to add the lye to the black tea. Stir carefully until the lye dissolves completely. The combination is probably brown, and that's good.
4. Mix your oils thoroughly and melt them. After the lye solution and oils have cooled to 130°C or below, mix them and stick until you have a thin trace.
5. You can add the fragrance oil once you have a faint trace.
6. Remove approximately 26 ounces of soap from the cup. Add two activated charcoal teaspoons and stir to blend entirely.
7. Add all the titanium dioxide and integrate well with the stick mixer in the enormous soap container. Split it into two, weighing around 26 ounces each.
8. You want to add the purple Brasilian clay to one-half of the mixture of titanium dioxide and add it to a stick blender.
9. Before you begin stacking, all soap containers need to be medium to thick.
10. You start by pouring in and stretching half of the uncolored soap equally but not straight.
11. Then put on the white soap, half black, but don't allow the first white layer to slip into the black soap. Spread it evenly and cover it with a spoon.

12. Finally, cover with a spoon with half the purple soap. To eliminate air bubbles, tap the mold hard.
13. Use the rest of the soap for a second time.
14. Use a spoon for the center and any other design that looks beautiful for you after the final purple layer.
15. Sprinkle on the top of the soap-dried black tea leaves and press gloves softly.
16. Spritz alcohol on top for soda ash prevention.
17. This soap should not be covered or isolated; cool. If you reside in a hot region, you can place the product in the fridge or freezer for several hours. Let the mold lie for 2 or 3 days or be removed easily.
18. For four to six weeks, cut into bars and heal

Energizing Coffee

Ingredients:

- Loaf Mold
- 13.9 ounces Olive Oil
- 8.3 ounces Coconut Oil
- 8.3 ounces Palm Oil
- 1.7 ounces Coffee Butter
- 1-ounce Coffee Oil
- 5 ounces Brewed Coffee
- 5 ounces Distilled Water
- 4.6 ounces Sodium Hydroxide Lye
- 2 Tablespoons Coffee Grounds
- Whole Coffee Beans

Directions:

1. While brewing your coffee, the darker the soap, the stronger the coffee has to be. It is best to use 5 ounces of brewed coffee when brewing.
2. Once the coffee has cooled to room temperature, add 5 ounces of filtered water to the mixture and stir to dissolve the lye.
3. Lye should be added to the coffee very gradually. The lye solution should be stirred well until it is entirely dissolved. However, this is very typical.

4. Once the oils have been combined and heated to a temperature of 130°F or more minor, allow it to cool.
5. Allow the liquid to cool completely, then mix in the lye and the oils until a light trace is reached.
6. When you have a medium trace, mix the soap and keep blending.
7. Make sure to thoroughly combine the coffee grinds into the soap using a whisk.
8. To ensure that no air bubbles in the soap, lay it in the mold before tapping it.
9. To create the required texture pattern in the middle of the soap, mix several colors in a controlled way.
10. Spread a layer of coffee beans across the soap mold. Gently press the beans in with gloved hands.
11. To avoid soda ash, spritz the top with alcohol.
12. Allow two to three days for the soap to cure in the mold before removing it.
13. Dry-cured for six weeks and then cut into bars.

Simple Orange Zest

Ingredients:

- Loaf Mold
- 33 ounces' soap making kit
- 10 ounces Distilled Water
- 4.7 ounces Sodium Hydroxide Lye
- Two teaspoons Sodium Lactate
- 1.7 ounces Orange Essential Oil
- Three teaspoons Orange Peel Powder
- Marigold Petals (optional)

Directions:

1. Mix lye and water slowly and thoroughly, stirring slightly until the lye is dissolved entirely.
2. Melt your mixer completely until no lumps or cloudiness is present. Also, if you don't want to utilize a kit, you may use your oil combination.
3. When the lye and oil are 130 degrees Fahrenheit, they may be mixed and added to sodium lactate at a lower temperature.
4. Wear a mixer with the stick and pulse the mix. Do this for 15-22 seconds, and then use the mixer to remove the mixture. Keep going until the soap reaches a thin pudding consistency.
5. Fill the soap with the orange essential oil and combine the aroma with the bonded mixer.
6. Add the orange peel and mix until no clumps are present and all is well integrated.
7. The soap should now be significantly thickened, and you want to continue blending until it is thick and can form peaks.
8. Put the soap into the loaf shape and tap the counter so that the air bubbles get released.
9. Create a peak in the middle of the soap or other design you choose with the help of a spoon.
10. Where desired, sprinkle on top marigold petals.
11. Alcohol splashes the top. Spritz.
12. Allow the soap to firm for 2 or 3 days in the mold or until the mold is readily removed.
13. Slice the soap in bars. Heal the bars four or six more weeks later.

Amber and Evergreen Soap

Ingredients:

- Loaf Mold
- 8.8 ounces Coconut Oil
- 8.8 ounces Palm Oil
- 8.8 ounces Olive Oil
- 3.5 ounces Meadow foam Oil
- 3.5 ounces Sweet Almond Oil
- 1.8 ounces Castor Oil
- 11.5 ounces Distilled Water
- 4.8 ounces Sodium Hydroxide Lye
- 2 ounces Cedar and Amber Fragrance Oil
- ½ teaspoon Yellow Oxide
- One teaspoon Evergreen Mica
- ½ teaspoon Burgundy Pigment
- One teaspoon Titanium Dioxide

Directions:

1. Get your colors ready. 1. Stir the titanium Dioxide and mix until the clumps are available with one teaspoon of liquid oil. Combine the yellow oxide & Burgundy pigment in separate containers with half a spoonful of your choice of oil until no clumps have been found. Finally, add one tablespoon of your selection of oils to the Evergreen Mica until no clumps are present.
2. Slowly and carefully mix water and lye and stir until lye is dissolved entirely and also the liquid is clear.
3. Mix the oils & melt fully. 3. When cooled down to or below 130 degrees Fahrenheit, they can be combined with lye and stuck until a thin trace is reached.
4. Split the soap into even four containers. Stir every container accordingly and mix it thoroughly:
1. You may use the two teaspoons of Titanium Dioxide to generate a white hue in a container.
2. Add 1⁄4 teaspoon in container two to the yellow color Oxide yellow.
3. Create green with all Evergreen Mica in container three.

4. I am adding 1⁄4 teaspoon of Burgundy pigment to container four to create the color red.
5. Add the fragrance oil evenly to all four containers and whisk to mix thoroughly.
6. You may use a stick blender and a pulse since each container is somewhat thick if the soap is still on an OK track. A light trace soap is best provided.
7. Have a big spoon for every color and put in three distinct places one color at a time into the mold.
8. In various spots, continue to plop the colored spoon into the mold. You can select how to do it, but don't twice lay the same hue. Tap the mold occasionally so that the air bubbles are removed.
9. Use chopsticks or dowels and place them at the top of the soap, then make S-shaped curves down the mold length and repeat them in the other directions.

10. Spritz the top of soda ash to avoid alcohol.
11. Cover the soap for 24hrs and permit it to sit for two or three days in the mold or extract it easily from the mold.
12. Slice into bars and let the soap heal for 4-6 weeks.

Honey Soap

Ingredients:

- Loaf Mold
- Bubble wrap to line the mold
- 1.8 ounces Argan Oil
- 1.8 ounces Castor Oil
- 7 ounces Coconut Oil
- 10.5 ounces Olive Oil
- 7 ounces Palm Oil
- 7 ounces Sunflower Oil
- 4.8 ounces Sodium Hydroxide Lye
- 11 ounces Distilled Water
- 2.3 ounces Honey Fragrance Oil
- One tablespoon Honey

Directions:

1. The completed soap will look like a honeycomb if you put your wick into the bottom of your soap mold. However, if you want to create a particular design in your soap or have a simple soap bar, you may also use an imprint mat; it depends on you.
2. Slowly and slowly add lye to the water and gently stir until the fluid is clear and the lye dissolves completely.
3. Mix the oils and melt. When the lye and the oils have cooled down to around 130 Fahrenheit, they may be combined and mixed until a bit of trace has come.
4. Add the sweetheart and stick to combine. Use the blender to mix and alternate between pulses.
5. Add the fragrance oil and swirl until well blended. Remove between pulses.
6. Keep blending until a mild trace is obtained.
7. Put the combination of soap into the mold and tap several times to scatter air bubbles.
8. Even the top with such a hopper and set it for 3 hours and up to twenty-four hours in the fridge or freezer immediately.
9. Let the soap be placed in your mold for two days, or remove the bubble wrap easily.
10. Cut into bars and let four to six weeks of healing.

Nettle, Spearmint & Lime

Ingredients:

- 20 ounces Vegetable Fat
- 6 ounces Coconut Oil
- 6 ounces Palm Oil
- 12 ounces Distilled Water
- Four ¼ ounces Sodium Hydroxide Lye
- One tablespoon Nettle Leaf Powder
- Dried Nettle Leaf
- One teaspoon Spearmint Essential Oil
- Two teaspoons Lime Fragrance Oil

Directions:

1. Add the lye cautiously and slowly to the water and stir until the lye is dissolved completely and the fluid is clear.
2. Mix the oils well and melt. When it is all cooled down to 130°F or less, you may mix lye with oils.

3. Once this trace has been reached, mix in the nettle, and remove a tiny bit of soap.
4. Turn it back to the bowl and mix quickly. Add the primary oils and stir thoroughly.
5. Fill the soap in the mold you choose.
6. Allow the mold to be set for 48 hours or removed from the mold till it is simple.
7. Allow it to heal for a few weeks, then moisten the top of the soap and massage into a dried nettle leaf. 2 to 3 weeks of treatment again.

Soothing Aloe Vera Soap

Ingredients:

- 7.5 ounces Distilled Water
- 3 ounces Sodium Hydroxide Lye
- 1.5 pounds Olive Oil
- 0.4 ounces Beeswax
- 1.8 ounces Aloe Vera Juice
- 0.18 ounces Mint Essential Oil

Directions:

1. Using a gentle and steady hand, add the lye to water. Once the lye has been dissolved, the liquid should be clear.
2. When the olive oil is heated to around 125 to 140 degrees Fahrenheit, add the beeswax little by bit.
3. Slowly add the lye mixture to the olive oil and stir until the mixture thickens.
4. When the mixture has thickened, stir until it starts to become sticky.

5. Add the essential oil and Aloe Vera Juice to the blender and mix until well combined. Stir with a whisk or spoon or for about a minute.
6. Submerge the soap mold in water and gently touch the side to remove air bubbles
7. Allow the mold to remain in a cloth for two days and then uncover. If the mold is giant, cover and let it sit for another day.
8. Allow the mixture to remain in the mold for another day before removing.
9. Allow to cure for one month and, from time to time, turn to keep the bars uniformly dry.

Charcoal and Bamboo Soap

Ingredients:

- 9.6 ounces Palm Oil
- 8 ounces Olive Oil
- 8 ounces Coconut Oil
- 4.8 ounces Palm Kernel Oil
- 1.6 ounces Castor Oil
- 1 Tablespoon of Charcoal Bamboo Powder
- 12.1 ounces Distilled Water
- 4.7 ounces Sodium Hydroxide Lye

Directions:

1. We are adding the lye cautiously and slowly. At the same time, stirring allows the solution to dissolve completely and the water to become transparent.
2. To make the blend trace, start by melting a small number of oils in a pot on the stove, then combine in the charcoal bamboo powder before adding the remainder of the oils.
3. If you like, you may add any fragrance oil of your choice and blend it until you get a smooth consistency.
4. Just sit down and pour into your choice of mold and tap on the top to clear the air for a few minutes.
5. Allow the product to remain in the mold for about 24hrs. Until it is easy to extract from the mold.
6. It takes six weeks to cure after it is cut into bars.

Tea Tree Oil Soap

Ingredients:

- 7.2 ounces Olive Oil
- 4.8 ounces Coconut Oil
- 2.08 ounces Sweet Almond Oil
- 1.92 ounces Avocado Oil
- 6.08 ounces Distilled Water
- 2.27 ounces Sodium Dioxide Lye
- 0.7 ounces Tea Tree Essential Oil

Directions:

1. Allow the lye to seep into the water as you gently add it. Ensure that the lye is thoroughly dissolved while stirring. When this occurs, the liquid becomes transparent.
2. Combine the oils in a glass or metal bowl and stir thoroughly.
3. The final temperature should range between 95 and 100 degrees Fahrenheit. Add the oils and lye gradually, blending with a stick blender until a very faint trace forms.
4. After that, add the tea tree and any other scent oils you desire. Assemble everything thoroughly.
5. Once the soap has hardened, place it in the mold and leave it for 24 hours or until it is easily removed.
6. Allow six weeks for the soap to cure before cutting.

Insecticidal Soap

Ingredients:

- One and ½ cups tallow
- ½ cup Coconut Oil
- ¾ cup Distilled Water
- ¼ cup Sodium Hydroxide Lye
- One teaspoon Citronella Essential Oil
- One teaspoon Eucalyptus Essential Oil
- One teaspoon Lavender Essential Oil

Directions:

1. Melt the coconut oil and the grease, put it away to cool.
2. Add lye to the water slowly and carefully and mix until it is completely dissolved.
3. When the oils and the lyes are 128 degrees F or more relaxed, mix them and mix.
4. Remove till creamy and thick. Remove.
5. Add essential oils and whisk for uniform distribution.
6. Fill in the molds you want. Tap Scatter Bubbles of Air.
7. Allow 24 to 48 hours or until the mold can be easily removed.
8. For 4 to 6 weeks, slice into bars and cure.

Lavender and Peppermint Antiseptic Soap

Ingredients:

- 16.91 ounces Coconut Oil
- 13.53 ounces Rice Bran Oil
- 3.38 ounces Sesame Oil
- 4.5 ounces Sodium Hydroxide Lye
- 10.48 ounces Distilled water
- ½ ounce Indigo paste or powder
- ½ ounce Peppermint Essential Oil
- ½ ounce Lavender Essential Oil

Directions:

1. Slowly and attentively add lye to the water, stirring until dissolved entirely.
2. Melt the oils and mix them thoroughly.
3. Fabulous oils and lye at or below 130 degrees and mix, mix till you achieve the trace.
4. In addition, add Indigo paste or powder, mixing with essential oils.
5. Put in the soap mold you choose, tap, and eliminate the air bubbles.
6. Allow 24 to 48 hours or remove the mold easily.
7. Cut into bars and heal for 4 to 6 weeks.

Soothing Chamomile Soap

Ingredients:

- 5.6 ounces Olive Oil infused with Chamomile
- 4.48 ounces Babassu Oil
- 2.4 ounces Coconut Oil
- 2.4 ounces Avocado Oil
- 1.12 ounces Cocoa Butter
- 2.33 ounces Sodium Hydroxide Lye
- 6.08 ounces Distilled water

Directions:

1. Slowly and sensibly add the lye to the water, gently stirring until dissolved.
2. Melt the oils and attempt to maintain the temperature below 100°C Fahrenheit to maintain the characteristics of the chamomile.
3. When the oil and lye have cooled, they may be mixed and blended until the desired trace is reached.
4. Add dried chamomile flowers and essential oils if desired.
5. Pour into the mold you want.
6. Place it for a couple of hours in the freezer to avoid the gel phase.
7. Allow the mold to set for 24 to 48 hours or to be removed from the mold easily.
8. Slice into bars and heal for 4 to 6 weeks.

Skin Blemish Soap

Ingredients:

- 8.8 ounces Shea Butter
- 2.4 ounces Palm Kernel Oil
- 2.4 ounces Palm Oil
- 2.4 ounces Coconut Oil
- 2.21 ounces Sodium Hydroxide Lye
- 6.08 ounces Distilled Water
- 1 to 2 teaspoons of African Black Soap Mixture

Directions:

1. Add the lye to the water very carefully and slowly and stir until dissolved totally.
2. Shea butter and oil melt and whisk together. Stir.
3. Let the oils and lye cool to 128 degrees Fahrenheit or less, stirring to trace.
4. Add the soap mixture to the desired texture.
5. Pour in the mold you want and tap to take the bubbles out of the air.
6. Allow the mold to be removed for 24 to 48 hours or until easy.
7. Slice into bars and heal for 4 to 6 weeks.

Chapter 6   Candle Making Recipes

General Beewax Recipe

Ingredients:

- 1 kg of wax
- Yellow wax coloring
- 5-10 drops of honeysuckle oil

Directions:

1. Prepare a wax by cutting or shaving.
2. Melt the wax with a water bath.
3. Add yellow candle wax and stir well.
4. Add a few drops of honeysuckle oil and stir again.
5. Optionally, if you choose your shape, cut the wick that has the same depth as the candle and about two inches more. Wrap the end of the wick around the pin (or similar) until the shape is balanced. The wick needs to

reach the bottom of the form (what about something that gives a touch of interest).

6. Slowly pour the melted wax mixture into a mold that must be placed on a flat surface and stored safely to prevent spills. Leave the wick and the stand (i.e., the pin) in place.

7. Set aside to cool and harden. It takes at least 16 hours, and it's better to leave for 24 hours.

8. Carefully open the cradle latch (e.g., pin) and then cut it to a quarter inch. A long wick means a more significant flame and a shorter life for your candle.

Banish Bugs Candle Recipe

Ingredients

- 1 kg of wax
- Green or emerald wax
- 5-10 drops of lemongrass oil

Directions:

1. Prepare wax by cutting or shaving.
2. Melt the wax with a water bath.
3. Add green candle wax and stir until blended.
4. Add a few drops of lime oil and mix again.
5. Optionally, if you choose your shape, cut the wick that has the same depth as the candle and about two inches more. Wrap the end of the wick around the pin (or similar) until the shape is balanced and the wick reaches the bottom of your form (maybe a ladybug or beetle will be fine).

6. Slowly pour the melted wax mixture into a mold that must be placed on a flat surface and stored safely to prevent spills. Leave the wick and the stand (i.e., the pin) in place.

7. Set aside to cool and harden. It takes at least 16 hours, and it's better to leave for 24 hours.

8. Carefully open the cradle latch (e.g., pin) and then cut it to a quarter inch. A long wick means a more significant flame and a shorter life for your candle.

Soothing candle recipes

Ingredients

- 1 kg of wax
- Chocolate or brown colored wax
- 5-10 drops of sandalwood oil
- 5-10 drops of jasmine oil

Directions:

1. Prepare a wax by cutting or shaving.
2. Melt the wax with a water bath.
3. Add the color of the brown wax and stir well.
4. Add a few drops of jasmine oil and sandalwood oil and stir again.
5. Optionally, if you choose your shape, cut the wick that has the same depth as the candle and about two inches more. Wrap the end of the piece long enough around the pin (or similar) to balance the shape. Allow the wick to reach the bottom of the form (the wood mixture matches a candle that resembles a large tree trunk).

6. Slowly pour the melted wax mixture into a mold that must be placed on a flat surface and stored safely to prevent spills. Leave the wick and the stand (i.e., the pin) in place.

7. Set aside to cool and harden. It takes at least 16 hours, and it's better to leave for 24 hours.

8. Carefully open the cradle latch (e.g., pin) and then cut it to a quarter inch. A long wick means a more significant flame and a shorter life for your candle.

Nurture Nature Candle Recipe

Ingredients

- 1 kg of wax (soy wax works fine here)
- Yellow wax coloring
- 5-10 drops of lemongrass oil

Directions:

1. Prepare wax by cutting or shaving.
2. Melt the wax with a water bath.
3. Add yellow candle wax and stir well.
4. Add a few drops of Citronella oil and stir again.
5. Optionally, if you choose your shape, cut the wick that has the same depth as the candle and about two inches more. Wrap the end of the wick around the pin (or similar) until the wick reaches its shape (maybe the scent of the fruit should be reflected in a lemon-shaped candle).

6. Slowly pour the melted wax mixture into a mold that must be placed on a flat surface and stored safely to prevent spills. Leave the wick and the stand (i.e., the pin) in place.

7. Set aside to cool and harden. It takes at least 16 hours, and it's better to leave for 24 hours.

8. Open the wick holder carefully (e.g., pin) and then cut it to a quarter of an inch - the long wick means longer flame and shorter candle life

Tropical Beach Candle Recipes for Parties

Ingredients:

- 1 kg of wax
- Yellow wax coloring
- 5-10 drops of coconut oil

Directions:

1. Prepare wax by cutting or shaving.
2. Melt the wax with a water bath.
3. Add yellow candle wax and stir well.
4. Add a few drops of coconut oil and stir again.
5. Optionally, if you choose your shape, cut the wick that has the same depth as the candle and about two inches more. Wrap the end of the wick around a pencil (or something similar) until the shape is balanced. The wick reaches the bottom of the form (how to use natural shells for authentic beach scents).

6. Slowly pour the melted wax mixture into a mold that must be placed on a flat surface and stored safely to prevent spills. Leave the wick and the stand (i.e., the pin) in place.

7. Set aside to cool and harden. It takes at least 16 hours, and it's better to leave for 24 hours.

8. Open the wick holder carefully (e.g., pin) and then cut it to a quarter of an inch - the long wick means longer flame and shorter candle life

Spicy Night Candle Recipe

Ingredients:

- 1 kg of wax
- Chocolate wax color
- 5-10 drops of ginger oil

Directions:

1. Prepare wax by cutting or shaving.
2. Melt the wax with a water bath.
3. Add the color of the brown wax and stir well.
4. Add a few drops of ginger and mix again.
5. Optionally, if you choose your shape, cut the wick that has the same depth as the candle and about two inches more. Wrap the end of the wick long enough around the pin (or similar) to balance the shape and allow the wick to reach the bottom of the form (the metal shape used to make truffles is a must here).

6. Slowly pour the melted wax mixture into a mold that must be placed on a flat surface and stored safely to prevent spills. Leave the wick and the stand (i.e., the pin) in place.

7. Set aside to cool and harden. It takes at least 16 hours, and it's better to leave for 24 hours.

8. Carefully open the cradle latch (e.g., pin) and then cut it to a quarter inch. A long wick means a more significant flame and a shorter life for your candle.

Feelings of the Forest Candle Recipe

Ingredients

- 1 kg of wax
- The color of the candle is green
- 5-10 drops of pine scent oil

Directions:

1. Prepare wax by cutting or shaving.
2. Melt the wax with a water bath.
3. Add green candle wax and stir until blended.
4. Add a few drops of pine oil and stir again.
5. Optionally, if you choose your shape, cut the wick that has the same depth as the candle and about two inches more. Wrap the end of the wick around the pin (or similar) until the shape is balanced. The wick reaches the

bottom of the form (maybe some wooden metal cookie cutters are the best idea).

6. Slowly pour the melted wax mixture into a mold that must be placed on a flat surface and stored safely to prevent spills. Leave the wick and the stand (i.e., the pin) in place.

7. Set aside to cool and harden. It takes at least 16 hours, and it's better to leave for 24 hours.

8. Carefully open the cradle latch (e.g., pin) and then cut it to a quarter inch. A long wick means a more significant flame and a shorter life for your candle.

Hive of Inactivity Candle Recipe

Ingredients:

- 1 pound of wax (obviously, the beeswax will work well with this soothing recipe)
- Yellow wax coloring
- 5-10 drops of honey-flavored oil

Directions:

1. Prepare wax by cutting or shaving.
2. Melt the wax with a water bath.
3. Add yellow candle wax and stir well.
4. Add a few drops of honey-flavored oil and stir again.
5. Optionally, if you choose your shape, cut the wick that has the same depth as the candle and about two inches more. Wrap the end of the piece long enough around the pin (or similar) to balance the shape and allow the wick to

reach the shape's bottom (the recipe only requires a honeycomb shape).

6. Slowly pour the melted wax mixture into a mold that must be placed on a flat surface and stored safely to prevent spills. Leave the wick and the stand (i.e., the pin) in place.

7. Set aside to cool and harden. It takes at least 16 hours, and it's better to leave for 24 hours.

8. Carefully open the cradle latch (e.g., pin) and then cut it to a quarter inch. A long wick means a more significant flame and a shorter life for your candle.

Scented Flower Candle Recipe

Ingredients:

- 1 kg of wax
- Blue candle color
- 5-10 drops of rose oil

Directions:

1. Prepare wax by cutting or shaving.
2. Melt the wax with a water bath.
3. Add the color of the blue wax and stir well.
4. Add a few drops of rose oil and stir again.
5. Optionally, if you choose your shape, cut the wick that has the same depth as the candle and about two inches more. Wrap the end of the wick around the pin (or similar) until the shape is balanced. The wick reaches the bottom of the form (another recipe that is suitable for the shape of the flower should not be a clear flower). The fragrance that the flower suggests is sufficient).
6. Slowly pour the melted wax mixture into a mold that must be placed on a flat surface and stored safely to prevent spills. Leave the wick and the stand (i.e., the pin) in place.

7. Set aside to cool and harden. It takes at least 16 hours, and it's better to leave for 24 hours.
8. Carefully open the cradle latch (e.g., pin) and then cut it to a quarter inch. A long wick means a more significant flame and a shorter life for your candle.

Butterfly Butter Massage Candle Recipe

Ingredients:

- 1 kg of wax
- Yellow wax coloring
- 5-10 drops of essential mango oil

Directions:

1. Prepare wax by cutting or shaving.
2. Melt the wax with a water bath.
3. Add yellow candle wax and stir well.
4. Add a few drops of mango oil and stir again.
5. Optionally, if you choose your shape, cut the wick that has the same depth as the candle and about two inches more. Wrap the end of the wick around the pin (or something similar) until the shape is balanced and the wick reaches the bottom of the form (as the name suggests, it must have a butterfly shape).

6. Slowly pour the melted wax mixture into a mold that must be placed on a flat surface and stored safely to prevent spills. Leave the wick and the stand (i.e., the pin) in place.

7. Set aside to cool and harden. It takes at least 16 hours, and it's better to leave for 24 hours.

8. Carefully open the cradle latch (e.g., pin) and then cut it to a quarter inch. A long wick means a more significant flame and a shorter life for your candle.

9. Note - Candles must be lit during the massage and not used as part of the massage.

Cinnamon Mulberry Candle

Ingredients:

- Wooden skewers or chopsticks
- Kitchen scale
- Stainless Steel Pans
- Thermometer
- Oven mitts
- Jar Containers
- Wicks
- Desired candle wax
- Desired colorant
- Mulberry Fragrance Oil
- Cinnamon Fragrance Oil

Directions:

1. Use glue to attach the wick to the bottom of the jars.
2. Measure the amount of wax you need to fill the jars, then divide it in half.

3. Melt each half of wax in its own container and add a separate color to each.
4. Leave the wax to cool to 130 degrees, and then add your desired fragrance oils.
5. Pour half of one color of wax into the container and let cool.
6. Pour half of the entire wax bowl into the half-full wax bowl and mix well.
7. Once a thin skin is formed on the top of the first layer, pour the second layer of mixed colors.
8. Leave the second layer to cool in the same manner as the first layer.
9. Pour the last layer.
10. Preheat the oven to 200 degrees Fahrenheit. Place the candle in for 5 to 10 minutes or until the top begins to melt.
11. Let the candle cool to room temperature in the oven.
12. Cut the wick to the desired length.

Summer Meadows Candle Recipe

Ingredients:

- 1 kg of wax
- The color of the candle is green
- 5-10 drops of clover essential oil

Directions:

1. Prepare wax by cutting or shaving.
2. Melt the wax with a water bath.
3. Add green candle wax and stir until blended.
4. Add a few drops of clove oil and stir again.
5. Optionally, if you choose your shape, cut the wick that has the same depth as the candle and about two inches more. Wrap the end of the wick around the pin (or similar) until the shape is balanced and let the wick reach

the shape's bottom edge (suggest the dome-like form of a clover).

6. Slowly pour the melted wax mixture into a mold that must be placed on a flat surface and stored safely to prevent spills. Leave the wick and the stand (i.e., the pin) in place.

7. Set aside to cool and harden. It takes at least 16 hours, and it's better to leave for 24 hours.

8. Carefully open the cradle latch (e.g., pin) and then cut it to a quarter inch. A long wick means a more significant flame and a shorter life for your candle.

Stars and Stripes Candle Recipe

Ingredients:

- 1/ 2 pounds of wax
- Coloring with red wax
- Blue candle color
- Candles light up
- 10-15 drops of blueberry scent oil

Directions:

1. Prepare half a kilo of wax by cutting or shaving.

2. Melt the wax with a water bath.

3. Add the color of the blue wax and stir well.

4. Add a few drops of blueberry flavor oil and mix again.

5. If you take a mold big enough to make a candle out of all the candles, cut the wick with the same length as the candle, about two inches more. Wrap the end of the piece long enough around the pin (or similar) to balance the shape and allow the wick to reach the shape's bottom (the recipe is best used when making thicker candles).

6. Allow to cool and harden for at least 16 hours.

7. Prepare the next half a kilo of candles by adding the blueberry flavor, but skip the coloring because this will be a white line.

8. Allow to cool and begin to harden. With rapid stirring, the newly formed crust melts and is then placed in a mold. Allowing it to cool will prevent the coating from melting the blue part of the wax, but it will soften enough to seal the two layers.

9. Allow to cool and harden for at least 16 hours.

10. Prepare the last half kilogram of the candle as described above by adding the color of the red candle and the scent of blueberries.

11. Allow to cool and begin to harden. With rapid stirring, the newly formed crust melts and is then placed in a mold. Just letting it cool prevents this layer from melting the waxy white cross-section. Still, it softens enough to cover the two adjacent layers.

12. Let it cool and harden for at least 16 hours.

13. Carefully open the cradle latch (e.g., pin) and then cut it to a quarter inch. A long wick means a more significant flame and a shorter life for your candle.

14. When finished, remove it from the shape and sprinkle glitter on a piece of wax paper. Warm the wax with a low hair dryer, gently wrap the wax, and the effect is complete.

Tropical Candle Recipe

Ingredients:

- 1 kg of wax
- Yellow wax coloring
- 5-10 drops of essential pineapple oil

Directions:

1. Prepare wax by cutting or shaving.
2. Melt the wax with a water bath.
3. Add yellow candle wax and stir well.
4. Add a few drops of pineapple oil and stir again.
5. Optionally, if you choose your shape, cut the wick that has the same depth as the candle and about two inches more. Fold the end of the wick around the pin (or similar) until the shape is balanced and the wick reaches the shape's bottom (perfect pineapple shape).
6. Slowly pour the melted wax mixture into a mold that must be placed on a flat surface and stored safely to prevent spills. Leave the wick and the stand (i.e., the pin) in place.

7. Set aside to cool and harden. It takes at least 16 hours, and it's better to leave for 24 hours.

8. Carefully open the cradle latch (e.g., pin) and then cut it to a quarter inch. A long wick means a more significant flame and a shorter life for your candle.

Ocean Breeze Candle

Ingredients:

- Wooden skewers or chopsticks
- Kitchen scale
- Stainless Steel Pans
- Thermometer
- Oven mitts
- Jar Containers
- Wicks
- Desired candle wax
- Desired colorant
- Ocean Fragrance Oil
- Storm Fragrance Oil

Directions:

1. Use glue to attach the wick to the bottom of the jars.
2. Measure the amount of wax you need to fill the jars, then divide it in half.
3. Melt each half of wax in its own container and add a separate color to each.

4. Cool the wax to 130 degrees, and then add your desired fragrance oils.
5. Pour half of one wax color into the container and let cool.
6. Pour half of the entire wax bowl into the half-full wax bowl and mix well.
7. Once the first layer of wax has a thin skin on top, pour the second layer of mixed colors.
8. Leave the second layer to cool in the same manner as the first layer.
9. Pour the last layer.
10. Preheat the oven to 200 degrees Fahrenheit.
11. Place the candle in for 5 to 10 minutes or until the top begins to melt.
12. Let the candle cool to room temperature in the oven.
13. Cut the wick to the desired length.

Orange Mint Candle

Ingredients:

- Wick bar or plastic straw
- Hot glue gun and hot glue
- Kitchen scale
- Pot for melting wax
- Thermometer
- Thin wire or wick pin
- Toothpicks
- Heat gun
- Oven mitts
- Clear containers
- Candle wicks
- Desired candle wax
- Desired concentrated liquid candle dyes
- Mandarin Fragrance Oil
- Spearmint Fragrance Oil

Directions:

1. Set the wick. Use the wick bar or straw to balance across the top of the container and keep the wick centered.
2. Put a dab of hot glue on the bottom of the wick tab. Then press to the inside center of the container bottom.
3. Melt enough wax to fill your container. Heat to about 180 degrees Fahrenheit.
4. Add your fragrance at 1 ounce per pound of wax.
5. Cool the wax to 150 to 160 degrees Fahrenheit and pour into the container with some space at the top. Ensure the wick is still in the center.
6. Allow it to cool until the wax is opaque on the sides with about ⅛ inch hard skin on top. About 30-35 minutes.
7. Using a thin wire or wick pin - place against the inner edge of the container and push to the bottom.
8. Do this until you have a ring of holes around the edge of the candle.
9. With a toothpick, add a tiny drop of liquid candle dye into each hole. Use a different toothpick for each color.
10. Take a heat gun to gently heat the top of the candle.
11. Next, heat around the side of the jar. Move evenly up and down a color hole for about 10 seconds.
12. The dye will continue to swirl. So once you are happy with the pattern, you should stop.
13. Allow cooling for about an hour.
14. Trim the wick to about ¼ inch from the top of the candle.
15. Allow curing for a couple days before burning.

Autumn Morning Candle

Ingredients:

- Wick bar or plastic straw
- Hot glue gun and hot glue
- Kitchen scale
- Pot for melting wax
- Thermometer
- Thin wire or wick pin
- Toothpicks
- Heat gun
- Oven mitts
- Clear containers
- Candle wicks
- Desired candle wax
- Desired concentrated liquid candle dyes
- Oak moss Fragrance Oil
- Fruit Slices Fragrance Oil

Directions:

1. Set the wick. Use the wick bar or straw to balance across the top of the container. Keep the wick in the middle.
2. Put a dab of hot glue on the bottom of the wick tab. Then press to the inside center of the container bottom.
3. Melt enough wax to fill your container. Heat to about 180 degrees Fahrenheit.
4. Add your fragrance at 1 ounce per pound of wax.
5. Cool the wax to 150 to 160 degrees Fahrenheit and pour into the container with some space at the top. Ensure the wick is still in the center.
6. Allow it to cool until the wax is opaque on the sides with about ⅛ inch hard skin on top. About 30-35 minutes.
7. Using a thin wire or wick pin - place against the inner edge of the container and push to the bottom.
8. Do this until you have a ring of holes around the edge of the candle.
9. With a toothpick, add a tiny drop of liquid candle dye into each hole. Use a different toothpick for each color.
10. Take a heat gun to gently heat the top of the candle.
11. Next, heat around the side of the jar. Move evenly up and down a color hole for about 10 seconds.
12. The dye will continue to swirl. So once you are happy with the pattern, you should stop.
13. Allow cooling for about an hour.
14. Trim the wick to about ¼ inch from the top of the candle.
15. Allow curing for a couple days before burning.

Log Cabin Candle

Ingredients:

- Wick bar or plastic straw
- Hot glue gun and hot glue
- Kitchen scale
- Pot for melting wax
- Thermometer
- Thin wire or wick pin
- Toothpicks
- Heat gun
- Oven mitts
- Clear containers
- Candle wicks
- Desired candle wax
- Desired concentrated liquid candle dyes
- Fireside Fragrance Oil
- Woodlands Fragrance Oil

Directions:

1. Set the wick. Use the wick bar or straw to balance across the top of the container. Keep the wick in the middle.
2. Put a dab of hot glue on the bottom of the wick tab. Then press to the inside center of the container bottom.
3. Melt enough wax to fill your container. Heat to about 180 degrees Fahrenheit. Add your fragrance at 1 ounce per pound of wax. Cool the wax to 150 to 160 degrees Fahrenheit and pour into the container with some space at the top. Ensure the wick is still in the center.
4. Allow it to cool until the wax is opaque on the sides with about ⅛ inch hard skin on top. About 30-35 minutes.
5. Using a thin wire or wick pin - place against the inner edge of the container and push to the bottom.
6. Do this until you have a ring of holes around the edge of the candle.
7. With a toothpick, add a tiny drop of liquid candle dye into each hole. Use a different toothpick for each color.
8. Take a heat gun to gently heat the top of the candle.
9. Next, heat around the side of the jar. Move evenly up and down a color hole for about 10 seconds.
10. The dye will continue to swirl. So once you are happy with the pattern, you should stop.
11. Allow cooling for about an hour.
12. Trim the wick to about ¼ inch from the top of the candle.
13. Allow curing for a couple days before burning.

Conclusion

I would like to know how this book could help you and if it gave you helpful knowledge. I know I can't solicit your valuable feedback directly, but I will undoubtedly keep the reviews section in mind. If you found this book helpful and learned something new and good, let me know. Through your reviews, I gain the confidence to do more for the world.

Now, it is time for us to part ways. I wish you an incredible journey ahead. I hope you have the best of luck.